» Small Group Reading

M000237311

Accompanies **Whole Class Teacher's Guide** pages 126–129.

Overview
People create a lot of garbage. But there are simple things people can do to reduce the amount of garbage they create.

Genre: Expository

Author: Alan Trussell-Cullen

Curriculum Link: Life Science

Word Count: 652

Number of Pages: 24

Materials

Lesson

Small Group Reading

- **Small Group Teaching Version**: Group 2 Book 26, *Garbage*
- **Student Book**: Group 2 Book 26, *Garbage*
- **Small Group White Board**

Independent Practice

- **Group 2 Worktext**: page 38, *Comprehension and Vocabulary*
- **Student Book**: Group 2 Book 26, *Garbage*
- **Rigby Intervention Fluent Reader™ Software**: Level K Passages
- **Other**: Notebook paper

Learning Objectives

Comprehension Focus	**Comprehension Strategy**: Infer **Genre Study**: Expository **Nonfiction Features**: Charts, Diagrams, Index
Skills Focus	**Phonics**: Silent Letter Consonant Pattern (*wr-*) **Fluency**: Use Punctuation to Inform Meaning **Vocabulary**: *landfill, pollute, recycle, reduce* **Vocabulary Strategy**: Use Synonyms **High-Frequency Words**: *more, most, places, problem, their, throw*

20 minutes — Week 6 Day 1: Session 2

Lesson

Teacher Materials	Student Material

Small Group Teaching Version Group 2 Book 26, *Garbage*	**Student Book** Group 2 Book 26, *Garbage*

Small Group White Board

Follow the lesson plan in the **Small Group Teaching Version** to teach the small group session.

20 minutes — Week 6 Day 2: Session 1

Independent Practice

Student Materials

Group 2 Worktext page 38, *Comprehension and Vocabulary*	**Student Book** Group 2 Book 26, *Garbage*

1. Students complete **Worktext** page.
2. Students reread *Garbage*.
3. Optional: Students answer writing prompt.
4. Optional: Students use **Rigby Intervetion Fluent Reader™ Software.**

Week 6 Day 1: Session 2

Lesson

1 Before Reading

- Preview the text.
- Build background.
- Set a purpose for reading.

2 Teach, Read, and Practice

- Teach skills at point of use: Comprehension, Phonics, Fluency, Vocabulary, High-Frequency Words, Genre, and Nonfiction Features.
- Guide students as they read and practice.
- Encourage students to discuss text with a learning partner.

3 After Reading

- Assess comprehension.
- Check predictions.
- Prepare for independent practice.

Week 6 Day 2: Session 1

Independent Practice

- Students will complete **Group 2 Worktext** page 38, *Comprehension and Vocabulary*. This page allows students to apply the comprehension and vocabulary skills taught in small group.
- Students will silently reread **Group 2 Book 26**, *Garbage*. As they read, students will practice making inferences.
- Optional: If they have time, students may use notebook paper to answer the writing prompt from Worktext page 38. This prompt encourages students to think deeply about the text.
- Optional: If they have time, students may use the **Rigby Intervention Fluent Reader™ Software**, with Level K Passages. This software offers students practice in fluency and comprehension.

Introduce the Book

Read the cover and back cover text and talk about the photographs.

Preview and Predict

Teach Preview: Nonfiction

- Tell students that good readers preview a book before reading it. Explain that looking at a book's title, table of contents, headings, pictures, and other features can help readers understand what the book will be about.

- *Good readers use previewing to help them think about what they already know about a topic. This will help them understand their reading better.*

Preview with Partner Have student pairs preview the book. Tell them to ask questions and make predictions about the book as they look at the title, table of contents, headings, pictures, and other features.

Make a Purposeful Prediction Tell students that they will use the information they found in their preview and what they know about garbage to make a prediction.

Turn and Talk *What do you predict happens to garbage after it's collected?*

Optional Sentence Frame: *I predict that garbage _____ after it's collected.*

GARBAGE

Alan Trussell-Cullen

Rigby
www.Rigby.com
1-800-531-5015

GARBAGE

Alan Trussell-Cullen

PAPER ONLY

Contents

Chapter 1 **So Much Garbage** 4
Chapter 2 **Transfer Stations** 8
Chapter 3 **Landfills** 14
Chapter 4 **Hazardous Waste Sites** 18
Chapter 5 **The Future of Garbage** 20
Glossary and Index 24

Build Background

Connect and Share

- Show students the contents of the trash can. Explain that at the end of every day, the trash can is emptied. Ask students what they think happens to garbage after it is collected.

- Draw a K-W-L chart on the **Small Group White Board**. Ask students to share what they know about garbage and write their responses in the K column.

- Ask students what kinds of things they want to learn about garbage and write their responses in the W column.

- Tell students that after they read the book you will fill in the L column with what they learned about garbage.

Set a Purpose for Reading

Let's read to find out where garbage goes after it is collected.

Teach

Nonfiction Feature: Charts

Introduce the Skill Point out the chart on page 5 and its heading. *The pie pieces help me understand what types of garbage make up a landfill.*

Apply the Skill

• Have students study the chart on page 5 and think about what the author wants them to know.

• *How can you use the chart to learn what type of garbage is found the most in landfills?* (I can look for the largest piece of the pie.)

Comprehension: Infer

Introduce the Skill Review the whole class instruction on inferring. *When we infer, we use what we know to deepen our understanding of what we read.*

Model the Skill Have students look at the picture on page 4. *I know that the garbage in my trash can often smells, so I can infer that the place in this picture smells, too!*

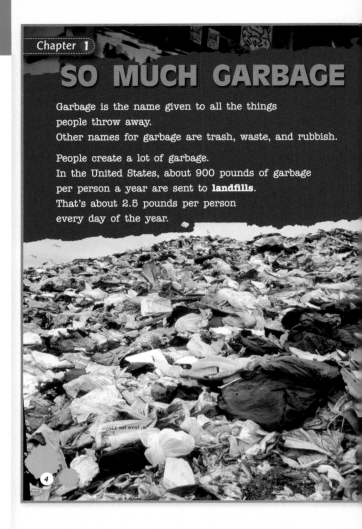

Chapter 1

SO MUCH GARBAGE

Garbage is the name given to all the things people throw away.
Other names for garbage are trash, waste, and rubbish.

People create a lot of garbage.
In the United States, about 900 pounds of garbage per person a year are sent to **landfills**.
That's about 2.5 pounds per person every day of the year.

Differentiating for ELLs

Levels 1–2
Have students point to the parts of the pie chart on page 5 that represent garbage people create in school and in their homes. Guide students to say the words on the chart, followed by the word *home* or *school*.

Level 3
Provide the sentence frames _____ *is garbage from schools/people's homes.* Have students make sentences using the words from the pie chart on page 5. If sentences are incomplete, model back to students a complete sentence embodying their meaning.

4 *Garbage*

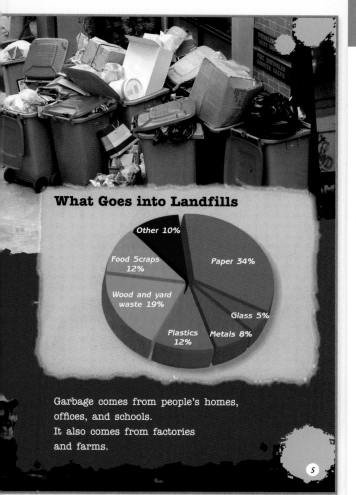

What Goes into Landfills

- Other 10%
- Paper 34%
- Food Scraps 12%
- Wood and yard waste 19%
- Plastics 12%
- Metals 8%
- Glass 5%

Garbage comes from people's homes, offices, and schools.
It also comes from factories and farms.

5

Comprehension: Infer

Guided Practice

- Tell students that as they read they should use inferring to think about the kinds of garbage that people create.

- Have students read pages 4 and 5 silently and at their own pace.

Turn and Talk *Think about what you read about the different places garbage comes from. What can you infer about the kinds of garbage people create in homes and schools?* **ELL**

Optional Sentence Frame: *I think the kinds of garbage people create in homes/ schools are . . .*

Extend Language To enrich language, brainstorm academic words to use, such as *disposable, scraps,* and *packaging.*

Levels 4–5

Have students answer the prompt using the words from the pie chart on page 5. Encourage students to provide examples using academic language, such as *tissue, carton, weeds,* and *wire.*

Build Vocabulary: *pollute*

Introduce and Explain the Word Have students look at the picture on the right-hand side of page 7. *When garbage is burned, it can pollute the air. To* pollute *means "to make air, water, or soil so dirty that it might be harmful to people or animals."*

Discuss the Word *What kinds of things can pollute a river? Share ideas with a partner.*

Fluency: Use Punctuation to Inform Meaning

Introduce the Skill

• Read page 6 aloud to students.

• *Notice how I paused at commas and then stopped at periods. Good readers use punctuation to read fluently and to better understand the text.*

The problem with garbage is finding the best way to get rid of it.

In most big cities, garbage is collected at the curb in trucks and taken to transfer stations.

From there, it may be sent to an incinerator to be burned, or it may be recycled or sent to a landfill.

6

Garbage is burned in incinerators at high temperatures. One problem with burning garbage is that the smoke may contain harmful chemicals that pollute the air.

A lot of the garbage collected can be recycled. More and more garbage is being recycled, but most garbage still ends up in landfills.

7

Fluency: Use Punctuation to Inform Meaning

Guided Practice

- Have students read pages 6 and 7 silently and at their own pace.

- Ask students to choose one sentence to read silently for fluency practice.

Apply in Pairs Have student pairs read their sentences aloud to each other several times.

Turn and Talk *Ask pairs to comment on their partner's reading.*

Optional Sentence Frame: As you were reading, I noticed that at the commas/ periods you . . .

High-Frequency Words:
more, most, problem

Introduce the Words

- Write *more*, *most*, and *problem* on the **Small Group White Board**. *You may have seen these words before.*

Guided Practice

- Tell students to write *more*, *most*, and *problem* on a piece of paper.

Turn and Talk Have student pairs practice spelling the words. Students should correct their partners if they make mistakes.

Genre: **Expository Text**

Introduce the Skill Tell students that expository writing informs, explains, or describes a topic. *Expository writing is organized into topics and details. Headings help readers find the topics, and the text provides more details about that topic.*

Model the Skill Point to the heading on page 8. *The main topic of this section will be transfer stations. As I read, I will think about what I'm learning about transfer stations.*

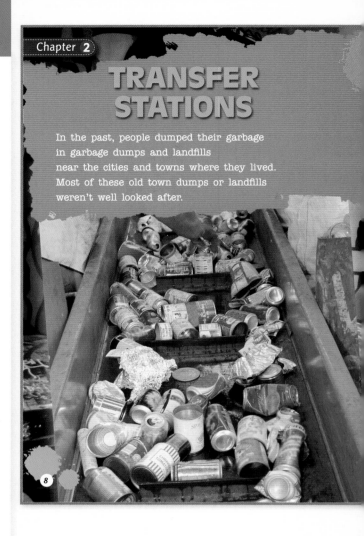

Chapter **2**

TRANSFER STATIONS

In the past, people dumped their garbage in garbage dumps and landfills near the cities and towns where they lived. Most of these old town dumps or landfills weren't well looked after.

8

They attracted rats and flies, and everything got dumped together, which meant harmful chemicals leaked out and poisoned the **groundwater**.

9

Genre: **Expository Text**

Guided Practice

- Tell students that as they read, they should pay attention to the details and use them to think about why transfer stations are important.

- Have students read pages 8 and 9 silently and at their own pace.

Turn and Talk *What is one detail you remember from your reading?*

Optional Sentence Frame: *One detail I remember from my reading is . . .*

Comprehension: Infer

Revisit the Skill Remind students that when we infer, we use what we know to deepen our understanding of what we read.

Model the Skill Point out the picture on page 10. *I don't see any buildings in this picture. I know that most cities have lots of buildings, so I can infer that the place shown in this picture is not in a city.*

Today land close to a city is too valuable to use for dumping garbage. Now garbage is taken great distances to more suitable places.

10

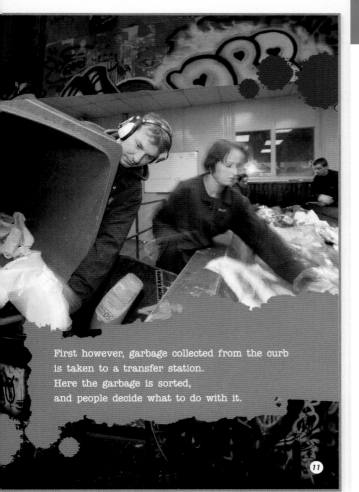

First however, garbage collected from the curb
is taken to a transfer station.
Here the garbage is sorted,
and people decide what to do with it.

11

Comprehension: Infer

Guided Practice

- Tell students that as they read they should use inferring to think about some reasons people might not want to dump garbage near a city.

- Have students read pages 10 and 11 silently and at their own pace.

Turn and Talk *Think about what you have read and what you know about garbage. What can you infer about why people might not want to dump garbage near a city?*

Optional Sentence Frame: *I can infer that people might not want to dump garbage near a city because . . .*

Extend Language To enrich language, brainstorm academic words to use, such as *pollution, germs,* and *odor.*

Vocabulary Strategy: Use Synonyms

Introduce the Skill Tell students that when they find a word they don't know, they should look for words that could mean the same as the unfamiliar word.

Model the Skill

- Read the first sentence on page 12 aloud.
  I wonder what hazardous *means. Let me look for other words that might mean the same as* hazardous.

- Read aloud from the top of the page.
  I notice that the text says that dangerous garbage is sent to a hazardous waste sight. Dangerous *and* hazardous *are both used to describe the garbage. I think* hazardous *means* dangerous.

Fluency: Use Punctuation to Inform Meaning

Revisit the Skill

- Read the first sentence on page 12 aloud to the students.

- *Notice how I paused at the comma and then stopped at the period. Good readers use punctuation to read fluently and to better understand the text.*

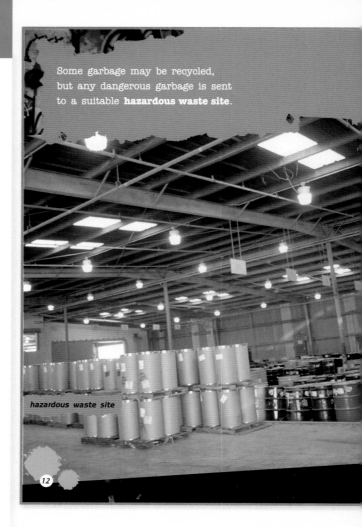

Some garbage may be recycled, but any dangerous garbage is sent to a suitable **hazardous waste site**.

hazardous waste site

12

The rest of the garbage collected at the curb goes through special machines that compact it so it doesn't take up a lot of space.
It is then taken by truck or barge to a landfill, which may be many miles away.

13

Fluency: Use Punctuation to Inform Meaning

Guided Practice

- Have students read pages 12 and 13 silently and at their own pace.

- Ask students to choose one sentence to read silently for fluency practice.

Apply in Pairs Have student pairs read their sentences aloud to each other several times.

Turn and Talk *Ask pairs to comment on their partner's reading.*

Optional Sentence Frame: I liked the way you _____ when you came to a comma/ period.

Build Vocabulary: *landfill*

Introduce and Explain the Word Have students look at the pictures. *These pictures show landfills. A landfill is a place set aside for people to dump trash.*

Discuss the Word *Would you like to live close to a landfill? Why or why not?* (ELL)

Optional Sentence Frame: *I would/would not like to live close to a landfill because . . .*

Genre: **Expository Text**

Revisit the Skill Remind students that expository writing informs, explains, or describes a topic. *Expository writing often has headings, diagrams, and photographs. Photographs help readers visualize what the author is trying to say.*

Chapter 3

LANDFILLS

A landfill is a large piece of land that has been set aside for dumping garbage.

14

Differentiating for ELLs

Levels 1–2
Have students draw and label a picture of what it would be like if their home was next to a landfill. Encourage them to use key words to explain why they would not like to live near a landfill.

Level 3
Have students draw and label a picture of what it would be like if their home was next to a landfill. Encourage them to use phrases and simple sentences to explain why they would not like to live near a landfill.

A modern landfill is specially built to store garbage safely. It is usually lined with plastic to make sure that any harmful chemicals left in the garbage don't pollute the groundwater.

15

Genre: **Expository Text**

Guided Practice

- Tell students as they read to think about how the photographs help them better understand the text.

- Have students read pages 14 and 15 silently and at their own pace.

Turn and Talk *How do the photographs help you better understand what the author is saying?*

Optional Sentence Frame: *The photographs help me understand what the author is saying by . . .*

Refine Predictions

Now that students have read some of the book, ask them to refine their predictions with the following prompts.

- *Based on what you have read so far, what happens to garbage after it is collected?*

- *Do you want to change your prediction based on what you read so far?*

Levels 4–5

Have students use complete sentences based on the frame above to convey their answer to the prompt. Encourage students to use academic language, such as *odor, sickness, disease,* and *germs.*

Nonfiction Feature: Diagrams

Introduce the Skill Point to the diagram on page 17. *A diagram is a drawing or figure that shows how something works or how it is made. The arrows and labels help you understand the different parts of the drawing and how they work together.*

Apply the Skill

- Have students study the diagram on page 17. Ask them to think about what the author wants them to know.

- *What does the diagram help you understand about the relationship between garbage and electricity?* (Garbage produces gas, which is burned to make electricity.)

Phonics: Silent Letter Consonant Pattern (*wr-*)

Introduce the Skill

- Write the letters *wr-* on the **Small Group White Board.**

- Hold up the board, point to the letters, and model saying the sound and a word that contains the silent letter consonant pattern (*write, wrench, wriggle*). *The* w *is silent. You only hear the* r *sound.*

Large landfills may take garbage from many cities and states, and sometimes even from other countries.

As sections of the landfill become full, they are wrapped and then sealed tightly.

16

gas is burned to produce electricity

gas from garbage collects in pipes

garbage produces gas

As the garbage inside breaks down,
it gives off gases.
Sometimes people at landfills collect the gases
given off by garbage.
The gases can be used to make electricity.

(17)

Read and Practice

Phonics: Silent Letter Consonant Pattern (*wr-*)

Guided Practice Have students repeat the sound of the *wr-* silent letter consonant pattern, and then model saying some other words that include the sound. Demonstrate writing these words.

Read and Apply

• Point out the *wr-* in *wrapped* in the last sentence on page 16.

• Have students read pages 16 and 17 silently and at their own pace. Remind them to look for opportunities to apply their knowledge about *wr-* as they read.

Turn and Talk Have student pairs take turns pointing out the wr words they found and reading them aloud (page 11: wrapped).

Teach

Comprehension: Infer

Revisit the Skill Remind students that when we infer, we use what we know to deepen our understanding of what we read.

Model the Skill Point out the picture on page 19. *This man is wearing gloves and a mask. I know that people wear these things to protect their skin and eyes from dangerous chemicals. I can infer that this man is working with dangerous chemicals.*

Background Building Tip

Explain that some hazardous waste comes from businesses, such as gas stations, dry cleaners, or hospitals. Tell students that other hazardous waste, like batteries, hair spray, and cleaning products, comes from people's homes. *Hazardous waste should be handled carefully because it can harm people and the environment.*

Chapter 4

HAZARDOUS WASTE SITES

Garbage from some factories may contain dangerous chemicals that cannot be dumped in an ordinary landfill. Some of this garbage is burned in incinerators, but most of it gets put in special places called hazardous waste sites.

Differentiating for ELLs

Levels 1–2

Write the words *food scraps, battery, wood, paint,* and *cleaning products* on the **Small Group White Board**. Draw a T-Chart. Label the left column "Landfill" and the right column "Hazardous Waste Site." Have students copy the T-chart on a piece of paper and sort the words into the proper columns. Encourage the students to say the words, assisting as necessary.

Level 3

Write the words *food scraps, batteries, wood, paint,* and *cleaning products* on the **Small Group White Board**. Provide the sentence frame _____ *is/are kept at a hazardous waste site.* Have students use the frame with the appropriate vocabulary.

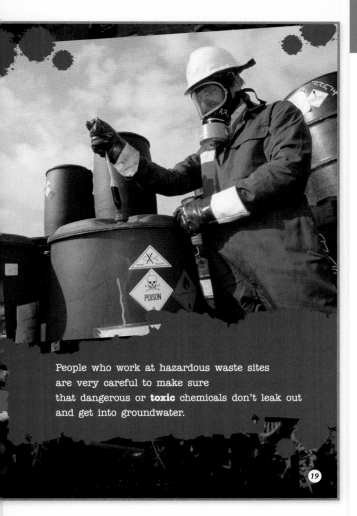

People who work at hazardous waste sites are very careful to make sure that dangerous or **toxic** chemicals don't leak out and get into groundwater.

19

Comprehension: Infer

Guided Practice

- *As you read, think about what you know about dangerous chemicals. Make an inference about why some garbage has to be kept in a special place.*

- Have students read pages 18 and 19 silently and at their own pace.

Turn and Talk *Why does some garbage have to be kept at a hazardous waste site?* **ELL**

Optional Sentence Frame: *Some garbage has to be kept at a hazardous waste site because . . .*

Levels 4–5

Write the words *food scraps, batteries, wood, paint,* and *cleaning products* on the **Small Group White Board**. Have students discuss which items should be kept in a hazardous waste site. Have them continue to brainstorm other types of garbage using academic language.

Build Vocabulary: *reduce*

Introduce and Explain the Word Read the last sentence on page 20. *To reduce means to lessen the amount of something.* Point to the picture on page 21. *Some people bring their own bags to the grocery store to reduce the number of plastic bags that are used.*

Discuss the Word *What are some ways people can reduce how much paper they use?* **ELL**

Optional Sentence Frame: People can reduce the amount of paper they use by . . .

Chapter 5

THE FUTURE OF GARBAGE

Many countries are running out of places to build new landfills.

However, there are some simple things people can do to reduce the amount of garbage they create.

20

Differentiating for ELLs

Levels 1–2
Write words such as the following on the **Small Group White Board**: *paper, dishes, reuse, recycle*. Help students use these words as they design a public service poster showing one way to reduce the amount of paper people use. Encourage students to share their poster with the class.

Level 3
Have students design a public service poster showing one way to reduce the amount of paper people use. Encourage students to share their poster with the class using phrases and simple sentences.

For example, every day Americans throw out
more than 11 tons of plastic shopping bags.
If everyone took their own bags to the supermarket,
it would save the cost of making all those bags,
and fewer plastic bags would go into the garbage.

21

High-Frequency Words:
places, throw, their

Introduce the Words

- Write *places, throw,* and *their* on the **Small Group White Board**. *You may have seen these words before.*

- Guide students to pronounce each word as you draw your finger beneath it.

Guided Practice

- Have each student choose one high-frequency word.

- Tell them to write a sentence using the word they chose but leaving a blank in place of the word.

Turn and Talk Have partners exchange sentences and try to guess the missing word.

Levels 4–5
Have students role-play a public service commercial showing one way to reduce the amount of paper people use. Encourage them to use complete sentences and elaborate on the details.

Build Vocabulary: *recycle*

Introduce and Explain the Word Have students look at the picture on the bottom of page 22. *This picture shows a place where people bring things to recycle. To* recycle *means "to put used objects or materials through a special process so that they can be used again."*

Discuss the Word *What kinds of things in your classroom can be recycled? Share ideas with your partner.*

Optional Sentence Frame: *I think _____ can be recycled because . . .*

Phonics: Silent Letter Consonant Pattern (*wr-*)

Revisit the Skill

- Write the letters *wr-* on the **Small Group White Board**.

- Hold up the board, point to the letters, and model saying the sound and a word that contains the silent letter consonant pattern (*wreck, wrinkle, wrist*). Review with students how the letters make only one sound because the *w* is silent.

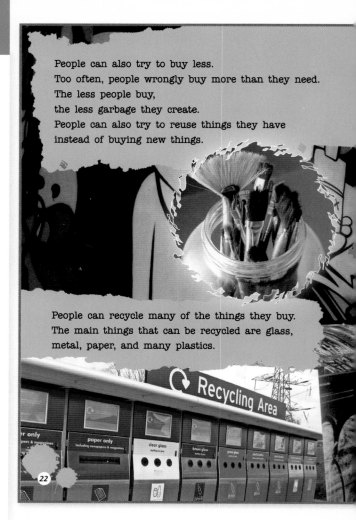

People can also try to buy less.
Too often, people wrongly buy more than they need.
The less people buy,
the less garbage they create.
People can also try to reuse things they have
instead of buying new things.

People can recycle many of the things they buy.
The main things that can be recycled are glass,
metal, paper, and many plastics.

22

Another important thing that people can do is to turn their yard waste and food scraps into compost.

Read and Practice

Phonics: Silent Letter Consonant Pattern (*wr-*)

Guided Practice Have students repeat the sound of the *wr-* silent letter consonant pattern, and then model saying some other words that include the sound. Demonstrate writing these words.

Read and Apply

- Point out the *wr-* in *wrongly* in the second sentence on page 22.

- Have students read pages 22 and 23 silently and at their own pace. Remind them to look for opportunities to apply their knowledge about *wr-* as they read.

Turn and Talk *Have student pairs take turns pointing out the wr- words they found and reading them aloud (page 22: wrongly).*

Background Building Tip

Tell students that *compost* is a pile of rotting material used to make garden soil richer. *Compost helps plants produce more leaves, flowers, fruits, or vegetables.*

Nonfiction Feature: Index

Introduce the Skill Explain that an index tells the page or pages where a reader can find key information in the text. *If you wanted to learn more about recycling, you would read pages 6 and 7, 12, and 22. In an informational text, you don't always have to read from beginning to end. You can choose the parts that are most helpful to you.*

Apply the Skill Have students practice using the index. *On what pages can I learn more about transfer stations?* (pages 6, 8, 11)

Glossary

groundwater	water under the ground
hazardous waste site	a place for dangerous garbage
landfills	places set aside for dumping garbage
toxic	poisonous

Index

chemicals 7, 9, 15, 18–19

compost 23

groundwater 9, 15, 19

hazardous waste site 12, 18–19

incinerator 6–7, 18

landfill 4–7, 8, 13, 14–17, 18, 20

plastic shopping bags 21

recycling 6–7, 12, 22

transfer stations 6, 8, 11

24

After Reading

✓ Daily Assessment Comprehension Check

Use the following questions to check students' comprehension.

- **Literal:** *What kind of garbage is stored at a hazardous waste site?* (garbage that contains dangerous chemicals)

- **Inferential:** *Why are transfer stations important?* (At transfer stations, people decide what to do with the different types of garbage.)

Check Predictions

Ask students to remember one of their predictions from the beginning of small group. *Was your prediction about what happens to garbage after it is collected accurate? What else did you learn about what happens after garbage is collected?*

Complete K-W-L Chart

- Ask students what they learned about garbage and write their responses in the L column of the chart.

- Discuss whether students still have things they want to know about garbage and didn't learn. Talk about ways to satisfy their curiosity—looking on the Internet, looking in an encyclopedia, visiting a local recycling center, and so on.

Prepare for Independent Practice

Prepare for Independent Practice Tell students that they will spend the next small group session working independently while you work with another small group.

Worktext, page 38

Comprehension and Vocabulary Practice
Garbage **Worktext** page 38: Students will complete this page first during the independent session.

Infer: Reread and Practice
Students will reread *Garbage* during the independent session. Remind them to think about making inferences as they read.

Optional:
Writing Prompt
Why should people reduce the amount of garbage that they create? (If there is less garbage, less land would be needed for landfills.)

Scaffold the Prompt:
Have students discuss what might happen if all of the landfills filled up.

Garbage

» About the Book
Look at page 13. What can you infer about why garbage is usually carried by truck or by boat instead of by car?

I can infer that trucks and boats are used to transport garbage because they are bigger than cars.

» Read Something New

A landfill is like a bathtub in the ground that holds garbage instead of water. A landfill shouldn't leak. If a landfill were to leak, garbage would pollute the soil and the water beneath the ground. To prevent leaking, soil is put over garbage in the landfill. The best kind of dirt for a landfill is blue clay. When blue clay mixes with water or chemicals, it hardens. The hard blue clay forms a shell around the garbage. This shell keeps the garbage from leaking.

» Answer Some Questions

1 If garbage were to **pollute** the land and water, people would become _____.
  a. happy **c.** sick
  b. bored **d.** healthy

2 What two words in the passage have the same meaning?
  a. garbage and soil
  b. dirt and soil
  c. ground and water
  d. bathtub and water

3 Based on what I know about bathtubs, I can infer that the bottom of a landfill is _____.
  a. smooth, with rounded edges
  b. bumpy, with rounded edges
  c. smooth, with sharp edges
  d. bumpy, with sharp edges

4 A **landfill** holds _____.
  a. water **c.** blue clay
  b. soil **d.** garbage

» Optional Writing Prompt

Why should people reduce the amount of garbage they create? Use your own paper to answer.

 38 Comprehension and Vocabulary   Group 2 Worktext

Optional:
Rigby Intervention Fluent Reader™ Software
Have students practice fluency and comprehension with Level K Passages. Students can record their reading of leveled passages and compare them to a fluent reader.